21st Century Tactics

Small Business Marketing Series
Book 2

By

Glyn Williams

More Books by Glyn Williams

'Small Business Marketing' Series

Book 1:
The 7 Deadly Sins of Advertising
(And How To Avoid Them)

(Amazon - http://bit.ly/7sinsna)

Book 2
21st Century Tactics

(Amazon - http://bit.ly/21stna)

Book 3
20 Great Marketing Channels

(Coming Soon)

Join Glyn's mailing list and read his business blog
(http://bit.ly/glynblog) for more great tips on sales & marketing

Acknowledgements

Huge thanks go out to Trevor Middleton for editing this book, to many business gurus for their wisdom and insight throughout the years including Nigel Botterill, Dan Ariely, Tony Robbins, Earl Nightingale, Brain Tracy, Malcolm Gladwell and hundreds more. Add to this the thousands of customers that I have dealt with over the years for allowing me to 'play' with their brains without their knowledge whilst testing various theories and approaches.

Notes

This book has been spellchecked by three different people, if you find any speeiling mistakkkes in this book then do let me know and I'll sack them, forcing them to live on welfare benefits forever :-)

For American readers, most words in which you use a 'z' it should really be an 's', (i.e. realize = realise, systemize = systemise) Don't argue the point because we invented the language :-) please check the correct queens english spelling before placing your complaint in an email to wetriedreallyhard@sorry.com

Table of Contents

Introduction

Those of you who have read my other books will know my approach. The advice and suggestions you read in the forthcoming pages are bullshit free. There is no fluff, no flowery language and no soft lessons to be learned here.

Those who do not know me should check out my other books listed on amazon here_(http://amzn.to/12fClLF) and my website at www.marketingformugs.com . There are a host of articles on there you will find useful as well as other resources you might like to use and find out about.

This is my second book, in the series 'Small Business Marketing'. My other book, 'The 7 Deadly Sins of Advertising' was written with the intention of helping you get more from your advertising spend. I will be referring to that book in several places in the coming chapters so save yourself the time and go and buy it...now! It will pay for itself many times over with your very first advertisement.

This book is *not* advertising-focused: it is *business-*focused. If you are a small business owner or you have decided to start a new business you will find lots of plain common sense; down to earth advice on how to make your business successful and – more importantly – how to keep it moving forwards.

I'll cover how you should start to evaluate your business, how you should plan it, and I'll reveal what you should be using day-by-day to market and promote your business as well as to how you need to run your business to stay alive.

Inside here are 15 well proven business practices that you will be able to implement. You don't have to be a brain surgeon to understand them, you just need the time to make them happen. I invite you to answer the question: "If I do not work on moving the business forwards, then who will? And what will happen as a result?"

We both know the answer. A business is either moving forwards or slipping backwards. There is no status quo where everything stays the same. Each day you are faced with new competitors looking to steal the business that you have for themselves. It's your job not only to stop them from taking it, but to take more for yourself.

Some of what you read within these pages may make you feel a little uncomfortable: for that I'm sorry but you might as well get used to it. The upside is that if you take heed of what I'm going to share with you then you will feel the euphoria of running a successful and profitable business.

If your business feels like it has come to a standstill then I can help. I can think of nothing worse than having a business that is stuck in a rut. Earl Nightingale once reminded us that a 'rut' is just a grave with the sides kicked out. If you find yourself or are in that position then I aim to help to get your business moving again on to greater things.

Why should you listen to me? Well, I've been a serial entrepreneur in my time. I ran and worked in two radio stations where marketing was our reason for existence, I've had a mail order empire for several years and I've worked at both ends of the business spectrum. In self-employment I've been a one man band and in corporate business I operated within the top levels of Rolls-Royce Aerospace as a communications expert.

Some of what you read will be established business practices looked at through new eyes; after all, just because time has moved on it does not mean that you approach everything differently. Many things will be new to you. All these tactics will help you as you forge your way forward.

Finally, and as part of my marketing for this book, At the end of the book is a link so that you can leave me a review. If you found this book useful then please leave a positive review as a review from you will help to give others an idea of what value the book can bring to them.

Enough waffle, let's get started

Plan to win

Do you have a business plan?

I'm not talking about an inch thick pad of A4 that you may have dragged to the bank when you first began.

That may be commonly called a business plan but in reality it's just a sales document for the financial lenders. Everyone in business will tell you that the only time you actually look at your business plan is when you are writing it, presenting it to lenders or having a review with your lenders.

The kind of business plan that I'm talking about is one that is a few sheets long at the maximum. It clearly defines for you and your staff exactly what your business is there to do, what services it provides, how it operates and how it makes money. It should be simple enough that you can show it your wife or even your mother-in-law and they can read it in less than 5 minutes.

You don't need reams of financial forecasts; you don't need huge in-depth marketing plans or profit & loss charts and contingency plans.

A clear short term plan will give you a constant yardstick with which to measure your business. It will give you clarity on where you are and where you want to go as you build your empire. Having a plan will keep you on track, a road-map if you like of your journey ahead. I urge you not to skip this step.

In this chapter we are going to get crystal clear on what your business is and what it plans to do in the next six months. Yes, just six months. Any further than that is pointless in today's business world as the landscape is changing at an exponential rate.

Also, if you plan more than six months in advance you will pour your heart and soul into that vision. What's more you will defend it and stick with it even if you know things are going wrong. The kind of plan we are going to produce is flexible, measured and easy to understand. A plan that you can pass on to others in your business, so that your employees also understand what you expect to happen.

Get yourself a large spiral notepad or open a word processing program on your computer. I often find that paper and pen are best when doing this as you avoid all the distractions of email, social media and the like.

Let's start your plan by answering some questions.

1) What business are we in - this will go at the top of your page 'XYZ Company is in the XXX business'

Wait though; before you do this make sure you know what business you are in. For example what business do you think the fast-food chain McDonalds is in? If you said 'food' then you are wrong. The actual business they are in is real estate: McDonalds buy or lease every plot of land that their shops are on and franchise them out. Their number one goal is to own as many pieces of land as possible. The food sales are secondary to their main business aim.

A local hotelier told me one day he was in the accommodation business, but is this really true? I'd suggest that he is in the entertainment and recreation business and the letting of rooms was just the catalyst to make that happen. Some hotel chains – for example Premier Inn*, The UK's largest hotel brand and Travelodge* – are indeed in the accommodation business, they're just boxes in a row with nothing else. *They know their business: do you know yours?* (*Before you say, they're both *owned* by companies with other business interests: they themselves, however, focus on that one key function).

So ask yourself the question above and then drill down to find out what business are you really in - what problem do you solve, what pain do you remove from your clients and what solutions do you give. What does the person or business using your service actually get from you? Add your answer to the top of a page of A4 now.

2) What are your channels to market for the next six months?

Where will people actually spend money? Here is the example for my company Marketing for Mugs:

Marketing for Mugs Channels to market: next six months

- Amazon bookstore

- Marketingformugs.com website

- Our email offers

- Personal appearances and presentations

- simonbozeat.com website (a business partner)

3) What is your mission statement?

In this part take two paragraphs to state your business ideals, your ethics, service and 'human' qualities that your business will have. Also list your number one mission. Here's an example of mine:

'We will provide down to earth, practical and usable information to small business owners to help them become successful. We will do this ethically and with integrity drawing on our own experiences and that of others. Our approach will be very down to earth, simple to digest and practical enough for our customers to act upon. We will act fast to rectify any problems the customer has with our products and services.

Our number one mission is to become the number one source of trusted business information and to be seen as the best of the best when it comes to business coaching and marketing advice for small business owners.

That's it, in a nutshell

4) How will we make money in the next six months?

List here every way that you will produce income. Do not be tempted to sit there and think of a thousand ways you will make money or you'll just overkill. Decide on no more than six and decide to thoroughly exploit those methods - here is an example:

- Book sales

- Publishing royalties from publishing for other authors

- Affiliate commissions from recommended products

- Personal appearance fees

- One-to-one coaching fees

- Twitter management fees

Note that each one of those actually pays money - not 'make widgets to sell' - making the widgets does not make money, selling the widgets on your website does. Make a very clear distinction on what you actually get paid for.

5. Which marketing channels will we use?

Choose the main channels you will use to generate traffic, leads and sales over the next six months. Just choose six to begin with and re-assess after three months. The key is to concentrate on those six, perfect them and then add more further down the line. Once you have decided on this do not be swayed by sales reps looking to sell you an advertising channel that you have not planned for. Remember, we are only planning the next few months.

Example of six marketing channels

- Twitter - personal and business account

- Facebook - Business Page

- A5 Flyers

- Local Newspaper

- Shop Signs

- Business Cards

I'm currently writing book number three which will be focused on some great marketing channels so keep an eye out for that one on my author page at Amazon. It may already be available by the time you buy this.

6. The Marketing Budget

Now you have decided on your marketing channels, decide how much money and time you will spend on each. Nothing is free, including Facebook and Twitter. All marketing has a cost and even if the actual thing itself is free – in the case of Twitter, say – your time is not free. We will address your time value in a later chapter.

Even with free channels you will find that there are tools you may need to make the most out of them. You may decide to pay for advertising on Twitter or Facebook; you may decide that you need extra software to run the accounts. Give a budget to everything in both time and money

Example

- Twitter - £200 for software + 1 hour per day

- Facebook - Business Page design £150 + 30 mins per day

- A5 Flyers - £100 for 5,000 + £50 for design

- Local Newspaper - £500 per month

- Shop Signs - £1200

- Business Cards - £100 for 500

7) Short term goals

From everything you have put in the rest of the plan you now need to define how you will measure your progress by defining some goals. Read what you have already written and determine the timeframe in which you will complete it.

Example

- Twitter account setup and in use with 200 followers - July 30th

- A5 Flyers printed and distributed - June 30th

- Three products on sale on website - June 30th

- Turnover £16000 by September 30th

You should then break these goals down into individual tasks - example

Goal: Twitter account setup and in use with 200 followers - July 30th

- Open Twitter Account

- Design logo

- Design profile page

- Learn about how to get followers

- Target followers and follow them

- Put links on our website

- Include links in email signatures

Do this for each of your goals and then reassess that the timeframe is realistic.

You will have many more goals than this of course and once they are all decided and broken down into tasks place them in chronological order.

Take the main goal title and date and print each one on large yellow circles of paper to stick on your office wall so they are in plain sight every day. Make sure you attach deadlines to every goal you have.

If a goal has no deadline it's just a dream!

Once you have done this your true 6 month business plan is complete, understandable and acts as a roadmap to get you where you want to be. Do be flexible though, review your goals every week and the entire plan every month. The key is to have a plan in the first place rather than just aimlessly wander around wondering what will happen next.

This approach makes you proactive rather than reactive. Proactive businesses plan for what lies ahead, reactive ones just react to whatever happens - they are fire fighters all the time and that approach leads to stress and sleepless nights.

It's your basic navigation system. Do not expect to be always on track. An airplane traveling from London to New York is off track for 90% of the time, the pilot makes small adjustments according the satellite navigation system every few minutes putting him back on course. You must learn to do the same and this plan will help to guide you.

Know your role

If you own your own business your role is that of a marketer.

Many will argue with this, if their company makes shoes they will say 'I'm a shoemaker' if their company is accountancy they will say 'I'm an accountant' but in reality neither of these statements is true.

If you are a business owner then your number one job is to get more customers and increase the business you already have from your existing customers. You may have to do other things within your business to service your clients and to deliver what they are purchasing from you; but marketing is your main job.

Nothing happens in any business without sales.

Many business owners enter into business because they previously worked for someone else. A joiner may start his own joinery company and decide to become a specialist in gates or doors or maybe windows. For years he has worked for an employer that has paid him to work which in turn earned the business owner money.

The joiner thought to himself 'why am I making my boss money? I can do this myself and keep the profit'. He then starts his own business with a handful of clients stolen from their employer and thinks that business will grow by word of mouth or on reputation. It doesn't happen like that and if it does to begin with then it very quickly dries up.

They forget the reason that they are the joiner and their employer was the business owner. The employer did not spend his time making doors and gates; he spent his time growing the business. I'm sure if you asked him that he would love to have spent time 'on the tools' making things with his hands, that may well be the reason he started in business; but as a business owner he quickly found out that his job was to get someone else to do the work whilst he marketed the business and made the money.

A lot of small business owners think they can delegate this task. They think that they can give someone else the full responsibility of sales and marketing so they can just concentrate on producing the end product whilst someone else gets the business. When they do this what happens? Yes, the sales and marketing guy eventually discovers that the whole business relies on him and that he is the one running it. It's very easy for this person to leave the company, start his own business and take your entire order book with him.

You have to take 100% responsibility for the business and that means taking 100% responsibility for the sales and marketing. Yes, you can have sales people working for you; yes you can have marketing people working for you but never *ever* delegate the full responsibility of the plan to market and sell your business to anyone else. No-one cares as much about your business as you do and they never will. This is a fact of life.

You must understand this core concept and accept that when you enter into business you are first and foremost a marketer, sales person and business owner. If you think you can run a business by doing the product / service work yourself and delegating the most important part to someone else then think again.

Nothing will happen in your business without a steady flow of new sales, that is your main job.

Action: Repeat after me... 'My Main Job Is ....'

The #1 key to success in business

There is one defining thing the separates those that run mega, super successful businesses from those that are the also-rans: the key to success in any business venture is finding the time to work ON your business rather than working IN your business. It's what you are doing right now whilst reading this book.

The most successful business entrepreneurs make time every day to work ON their business rather than working IN their business. Let's define that for a moment.

Working IN your business is the day-to-day running of the business. The dispatch of orders, the emailing of customers and suppliers, the placing of orders, the manufacturing and actual delivery of the product or service that you provide, ordering stock etc. That is working IN your business.

Working ON your business is doing your number one job. It's planning the marketing and expansion of your business. It's discovering new ways of attracting customers, it's reading books, taking courses, planning and doing. In a nutshell it's all about expansion and working smarter rather than harder.

The best of the best when it comes to building successful businesses make time for this every day. Nigel Botterill, founder of not one, but *eight* million pound businesses in the UK does it, Richard Branson, the UK's most famous billionaire and founder of the Virgin group does it and you should do it too.

The way that most do it is to make sure they spend an allocated slice of time, every day, purely working ON their business. Botterill prescribes that the first 90 minutes a day should be spent ON your business, others make do with an hour, and some do two hours. It doesn't matter how long you do this for as long as you make it highly focused time where you do nothing else. You close your email program, you turn off your mobile phone, and you lock yourself in an office or take yourself out of the day-to-day working completely. All you do during this time is work on moving your business forward.

If you resolve to do 90 minutes a day then in a four week period you will have spent the equivalent of a whole working week working purely ON your business. How powerful do you think that will be?!

It's important to make it routine. Given that this is the most important thing you do in your business, it makes sense to do it at your most productive time of the day. For most that is first thing in a morning.

Not only should you plan this time, you should plan what to do with it. Spend the very first session planning what to do with your forthcoming sessions! That is a good use of the time. Write yourself a to-do list of all the things you want to do whilst working ON your business. These chunks of time will form the basis of your business.

Here's an example to-do list:

- Investigate pay-per-click (ppc)

- Open a Google Adwords account

- Plan a ppc campaign

- Plan an email campaign

- Find out about banner retargetting

- Write some copy for my next advertisement

- Plan out the year for local newspaper adverts

- Decide on a solid way to measure my results

- Research a new product line

- Write an article or book

- Look into text marketing and decide on a plan

The list is endless, you won't run out of things to work on in your alloted time and all this activity will move your business forward. Use a ring bound A4 pad for your work and you can then look back easily on what you were working on to jog your memory. A paper spiral bound book is so much better than having to grapple with a computer: it doesn't break down, and if your pen doesn't work then you just pick up a new pen and away you go. Sometimes old school is best.

Action:

Decide how long you will spend each day, what time of day it will be (the start of the day is usually best) and how you will make this time distraction free. Make this a firm, immovable commitment.

Spend your very first session brainstorming all the things that you want to do to move your business forward, write every single one down and then choose your top ones to make a short list for your first week. As you did in the business plan earlier, break these down into tasks and consider which of these tasks you can delegate to others.

Then simply start doing it. Make sure everyone knows this is your time and you are not to be disturbed no matter what. If this is a problem then go out to a local hotel, order some coffee and find a quiet corner in which to work.

If you do this every day at the beginning of the day you do two things: first you put in place a habit that will pay you dividends for years to come and secondly you get to do your most important job first thing every day. If you really want your business to be a success you MUST do this.

What is your time worth?

Just how much is your time worth?

This is a very important question to ask yourself. If you know what your hourly rate needs to be then you know that you should not be spending time on activities that you can buy in cheaper than you!

Set yourself a target of your annual earnings; let's say for example you want to earn 150,000 in the next 12 months.

Take that figure and divide it by the number of working days in a year - around 200 after holidays and the like. $150,000 / 200 = 750$ per day.

Divide that figure by the number of productive hours you have in a day - for me it's about 7 after lunches etc $750 / 7 = 107.14$ - that's how much my time is worth.

So what do you do with this information? If your time is worth 107 per hour then why would you spend time on activities that you can buy in cheaper? Designing flyers for example is a service you can buy in cheaply; answering the phone can be done by a virtual assistant.

A virtual assistant (VA) is a great investment. These are people that work from home and charge you by the hour. There are websites such as elance.com where people in countries all across the world offer their time for you to buy. You only pay for the time you use and they are cheap - often less than $6 an hour.

This then frees you up to do the important things in your business.

There are other ways you can save your time. Email for example only really needs checking twice a day - once in the morning and once at around 4pm. Nothing is so important in email that it cannot wait.

Action: Work out what YOUR time is worth using the calculation above and then decide if it is realistic. You may calculate as many times as you wish but before you carry on with this book you must settle on a figure.

Build Your Personal Gold Mine

Wherever you read a book on Internet marketing you will find the phrase 'The money is in the list' and it's true. But it's also true in all forms of marketing – including yours.

During the early 2000s, when I ran a mail order business on the Internet, I used eBay, QXL and various other auction websites and I also ran several of my own. My list comprised of those people who had bought something from me. It was not a list of people who had asked for a free report: these people were *already* my customers.

Whenever I needed to make some money fast I would craft an email to my list with some kind of offer and I just knew it would generate some income. Sure as eggs were eggs within a few hours I had new orders. I would use this list at least once every two weeks to generate income that I would not have otherwise had.

Your existing customers are your very own gold mine. It is proven to be six times more difficult to get sales from a new customer than it is to sell an existing customer. People that have already bought from you simply know, like and trust that you will deliver on your promises; they are easy to sell to and love to buy.

So many businesses do not make the most of this and spend all their time working hard to find new customers when they have a ready made source of income from existing ones. Why is this?

Many fear that by continually asking for business from a customer that they will somehow annoy the customer and they may go off you. Why on earth would you think this? They have already bought from you and the only reason you have them on your list is to sell to them again. If you do not want to sell them anything again then what's the point of having their name on there?

Even customers that may have had a poor experience with you may buy again. I used to sell radio advertising on a small local station. There are many factors that affect whether a radio commercial will work or not. The words in the commercial, the music, the time of year, the audience, the time of day the commercial is played – so many things to get right or wrong.

People that buy from you know that you don't always get things right. If that were true then every radio commercial ever written would be a roaring success. I've written commercials that have resulted in millions in extra revenue for businesses and I've written commercials FOR THE SAME CLIENT that did not earn a bean. Sometimes you just get it wrong (sometimes you get it ALL wrong)

I've written commercials for companies that had not one single lead from it, I've gone back to that company and sold them again and had success. If you allow past dealings to influence your marketing to those companies then you are leaving money on the table. I leave clients on the list even if I have had to take them to court to get paid!

One of my customers ran a furniture shop. The commercial ran and was a small success for the client – his problem was his location and it was difficult to motivate prospective clients to travel to the store. We did it by working on a very special offer that was not available anywhere else. After the campaign I had to take the client to court to get paid. Six months later he responded to an email campaign and we did another deal together. This time it was cash up front of course but the point that I'm making is that the deals are still there even when the previous deal was sour. You just find a way to avoid the bad experience happening again.

The client opened another business after that one, and we had dealings a further four times after that. Don't allow yourself to hold on to grudges: 'It's just business' as they say in The Godfather.

If you are not collecting customer data then you absolutely positively must start now, you are leaving piles and piles of money on the table for other people to take. Remember this; the money is being spent, if it's not being spent with you then its being spent with your competitors.

So, what information do you need? Their names,

addresses, phone number, email, and a note of what they have already bought from you. When you have this information you need to get it transferred into a simple to use system that you can use regularly to market to those customers. You can't have too much information. As you start to learn to use your CRM (customer relationship management) system you can segment your customers into groups and target them really well.

There are several CRM Systems available on the market including a few that are totally free. Zoho CRM (www.zoho.com) is one such online CRM system that costs nothing, allows you to send emails with attachments and keep all of the information that you need. Then you could go up all the way to Infusionsoft, which is the CRM that all the big money marketers use. It's not cheap though, at several hundred a month. Start small with a free CRM and you can expand as you need. The important thing is to start, don't put it off.

You must also find a way to collect that information. A simple postcard can do the job with the offer of a prize draw for the customer filling it in. Take that information and get your assistant to put it into your CRM database and before you know it you will have hundreds of contacts that you can market to. You need a form on your website too and even on your Facebook page if you have one to capture people that are interested in what you offer.

Not all contacts are equal, collecting emails and names from people with an interest in what you do is a good thing to do but the gold is in the list of people that have already bought. Remember: it is six times easier to sell them than it is to sell a new customer.

You will then have what we call a targeted list. You can use this list in your marketing channels such as email, direct mail, postcards and more.

Action:

- Set yourself up with a CRM system

- Populate CRM with your customer base

- Start collecting information from your customers and prospects

How to make more money from each customer

Getting customers to buy from you is hard work. You do all the sales and marketing and you get the customer interested and then you sell to them. That is often quite a long process where the prospective customer has gone through a buying cycle. When they eventually do buy then there's a way that you can make more money and makes the most of your marketing investment.

The easiest time to sell someone something is when they have just bought something. Think about this; let's take the example of a car buyer. They take the test drive, read all the reviews, buy the magazines and eventually get to the point where they are ready to buy a car. Does the salesman sell them the car and then let them just walk away? You know that they don't.

Car sales franchises are very savvy at extracting the most from their customers. Once the buyer has made the decision to buy it is time for the UPSELL. 'Would you like the upgraded radio sir? The special go-faster stripes? The running lights, the 'peace of mind' warranties'

Upselling is the art of asking yourself what else can you sell this person and then asking them.

Many salespeople are scared of upselling, they think that it could tip the scales against the original deal and the buyer could back out - this does NOT happen; in fact the opposite is true. Having made a decision to buy the customer has psychologically and emotionally committed to the sale. He has told you that he is willing to go ahead and it's extremely rare that he will go back on that decision now he has committed. Once you have a 'yes' then it's time to get more.

To make the most of each and every selling opportunity you must embrace the concept of the upsell and teach this to everyone in your company. You and your staff need always to be thinking: 'what else does the customer need that he can buy from us?'

Let's take an example or two.

In food sales the fast food outlet should always say 'would you like to super size that?', 'would you like a soft drink with it?' 'Is that a large soft drink?' 'Have you seen our offer today of a free shake with two super sized meals?'…and so on. This is all upselling and getting more from each customer.

A carpet store to a customer that has bought a new carpet might ask 'Would you like the luxury backing?' 'Would you like the express fitting option?' 'How about stain guard?' 'UV Protection?' 'Would you like us to turn the offcuts into rugs for you?'

A pet shop selling tropical fish: 'Would you like some plants?' 'Do you need any fish food?' 'Have you conditioned the water lately? We have an offer on water conditioner today'

A hardware store selling a power drill: 'Do you need wall plugs? Screws, Drill bits?' 'We have an offer on that model where you save £10 on a new jigsaw cutter, would you like one?'

Simply asking the question of the customer: 'What are you going to use this for?' opens up your mind to other possibilities. The car buyer may be buying the 4X4 for off road use, so: 'We have specially branded 'Range Rover' wellingtons, would you like some?'

Upselling is the single most powerful way of increasing your business sales. You have worked hard to get that customer to buy from your business, working that little bit smarter and always going for the upsell can literally double or triple your turnover.

If you are at all unsure about this then think about when you bought something, and purchased 'extras' did it put you off the original decision?

Action:

Learn to Upsell - always consider 'what else goes with this product / service that I can provide?'

The Compelling offer

When I was selling advertising I met literally hundreds of small business owners. A fair proportion of them had totally the wrong idea when it came to 'special offers'. Many would say to me 'Glyn, I don't want to do a special offer - it's too 'salesy' for my business. I provide a good service / product and it just doesn't sit right with me. Can we do it a different way?'

If you think that offers are too 'salesy' and there is something not right if a company has to make an offer then think again. To attract people to buy and to buy NOW you must have an offer. If you don't have an offer then you are losing out to the next company they go to because they DO have an offer.

There is nothing morally or ethically wrong with making an offer. By making an offer you are doing the customer a service allowing them to get something they would not normally get at a discount. Answer me this, what's wrong in giving the customer a great offer?

The biggest companies in the world do offers, just go into your local supermarket and see how many there are. 'Buy one get one free', 'Half price today', 'buy this cheese and get a free half bottle of wine'. These companies know that it gives them an edge in the market.

Yes it's 'salesy' and it should be - you need sales!

Your offer is a compelling reason for someone to buy your product. But how do you make an offer?

A Good Offer Should Make You Money, Not Cost You Money...but how do you do that?

Let me illustrate the point with a personal story that I've shared before.

My wife of 30 years religiously goes to the hairdresser every Saturday. It's almost a ritual with her. She loves her 'bling' and loves to feel good about herself. Having her hair and nails done is all it takes so who am I to argue?

Anyway, last Saturday was 'colour week' – around every four to five weeks she has a colour applied to her hair and it's a good 90-minute job (the ladies reading this will be well aware)

The salon she uses is a quite high end one for our area. It's clean, well managed and they are ALWAYS upselling the services they provide. You may think that they are expensive but in truth although it *feels* expensive they are only a few pounds more than any of the competition.

The place is super clean, has good signs and it feels like it's a place to be pampered. Upon entering the salon her coat is taken by someone on reception and hung up carefully and they make her a really nice cappuccino (I know as I've had one too), which all adds to the feeling that she is in a quality salon.

Last Saturday when I arrived to collect her from the salon she came to the car with a small box in her hand. She looked at me with a beaming smile and asked 'do you like my hair?' As usual I complemented her on the look and said she looked great. She was genuinely excited this time though, although the overall effect was just as good every week it was clear that she felt a little more special this week.

'I've had a free treatment' she said 'It feels really silky and smooth today – They put this stuff on my hair' At this point she revealed a glossy box with a spray in it. 'Bet that was expensive' I replied, just like most men; 'No!' She said, 'because I had a free treatment with it **and I saved two pounds on the bottle!'**

The bottle of spray was a branded one from a company called GHD – again ladies will most likely recognise that brand as one of the best in straighteners, dryers and tongs. They've now branched out into haircare products too.

'The bottle was usually seventeen pounds, but I got two pounds off and they gave me a free treatment' she said. To her the two pounds off and the free treatment was a bargain to be had. Think about that… just two pounds to make a customer happy.

What a great offer that was. For the sake of £2 and probably 10p's worth of their own serum from the bottle they made an offer that many customers found irresistible. The client got a good deal, bought something they would not have known about, felt a million dollars and the salon increased the sale from that client by £15 – that's about 20% more than she would normally spend.

Now that's a good offer – It made the salon money and didn't cost them money.

The short-sighted salon owner would say they had lost money because they didn't get the correct retail price of the product. What they miss out on is that the sale would never have taken place without the offer. Even if the bottle cost price was £10 it was more profit in the tills.

You should now be thinking how can you use this in your business? What are people buying in your business right now that has a complementary product that they don't normally buy? How can you implement this 'upsell' approach with a compelling offer, right at the point where your prospect is buying? What else can you sell them?

The salon knew their customers; they knew what they wanted and how they wanted to feel. This particular upsell was broad enough in appeal to be transformed into an offer campaign - they knew that large numbers of women would respond to the offer and so they launched a campaign. The campaign was 'free GHD Silk treatment this month'. They tweeted it, posted it on Facebook, emailed their client list, took out a quarter page in the local newspaper and also used text messaging out to their existing client base.

When you put an offer together please resist the temptation to go for the X% money off: it's idle marketing and rather than making you money it loses you money. Instead think to yourself how can I add value to the customer and charge a little more?

You should change your offers regularly; large retail stores have worked out ways to have massive discounts on large items. Take for example a retailer selling beds – they have a large range of unique beds and so can do this – they will take say six beds and double the price for three months. They aren't expecting to sell any but may well do as an added bonus. In three months they reduce the price back to the same price they had before and run a 50% off sale on those models. Does it work? Every day in every city in the world.

Some businesses think this is wrong, I disagree. Value is relative to the customers' expectations. There is a science as to how we reach the value of something: if you want to look into this I'd recommend reading 'Predictably Irrational: The Hidden Forces that Shape Our Decisions' – an excellent study into human behavior when it comes to pricing and rewards. A link to the book is on my recommended reading page at marketingformugs.com

Three months ago they were selling beds at say £300 - they were not selling. The doubled the price and then halved it back to £300 and sold lots - what's wrong with that?

Action:

Give them a compelling reason to buy! - ALL THE TIME

Self Sabotage
(Don't shoot yourself in the foot)

I live in a beautiful part of the UK called Derbyshire. We are surrounded by countryside that is awe-inspiring and enjoy many days out in our convertible car with the top well and truly down, the wind flowing through our hair.

This past weekend we decided to visit Chatsworth House, a stately home right in the middle of Derbyshire with acres upon acres of beautiful scenery. We enjoyed a leisurely stroll by the river. If you ever find yourself in Derbyshire then I thoroughly recommend a visit, you'll love it just as much as my wife and I do.

After the stroll and a leisurely drive around we decided to visit the Chatsworth Farm Shop. They sell lots of the estate's own produce plus fruit and vegetables and it's very high quality produce.

The people that run the Chatsworth estate are very astute in business; wherever they can they will find a way of extracting money from your pocket. At several locations on the site they have tea rooms in which you can order drinks and snacks, all of which are produced on the estate. The Farm Shop also has its own tea rooms.

The sun was belting down on Sunday so we decided to have a cup of tea and a muffin outside the restaurant on a patio area. The paved area was full of tables but they were all occupied. There were, however, some stone benches just a few feet further forward from the tables so we thought 'that will do' Below is a picture of the area. You can see on the left the seating tables and to the right where the benches are.

We went inside to order our goodies and were met with a chain across the doorway 'Please wait here to be seated' read the sign on the chain. We did as instructed and a waitress came over to us removing the chain:

'I'll find you a table' she said.

'That's ok sweetheart, we don't need one as we are going

outside'

'You can't!' she snapped: 'the tables are all full'

'That's fine, the benches next to the wall will be okay for us' I smiled

'No, we can't serve to that area' again she snapped at us

'Why not?' I asked

'Our insurance won't cover us for breakages' – a lame excuse that appeared quickly made up to defend her entrenched attitude.

'If we break the cups then I'll pay' I said.

She was having none of it, and her attitude was awful. The paved area and the bench area had exactly the same flooring around it but was outside of the chain fence around the tables. For us to buy a drink we had to either take a table inside or wait for a table outside to become free.

What we did was go outside and leave the tea rooms entirely with a resolution never to go to the tea-rooms or indeed the farm shop again. We had dirty looks from the member of staff as we left. Our money stayed in my pocket and not in their tills.

Does your business have sabotage points like this?

Putting rules in place that alienate customers is never a wise thing to do. Customers are your lifeblood; your business exists purely to serve them. So many businesses take the opposite approach: 'if they want to do business with us then they will do it our way!'

Check to make sure that your staff understand that the customer is king: they have money in their pockets and it's you staff's job to get them to give it to you. Wherever you spot this kind of sabotage make sure you stamp it out immediately. Once it's been done it can cause irreparable damage to your business. You never know who the customer is; they could be a TV presenter, a news reporter or even an author that will use their sloppy business as an example in a book. A bit like this one perhaps.

Here's another example of how you could be sabotaging yourself.

On a similar day out we decided to eat lunch in a country tavern called The Coopers Arms. The Sunday lunch was a carvery. For those who have not experienced a carvery it is basically a serve yourself system where the restaurant puts the meat on your serving plate and you choose your own vegetables, sauces etc.

'What is the cost of the carvery' I asked. I was told that it all depended which meat you wanted and was shown a menu. There were around seven choices: Lamb, Beef, Pork, Turkey, Vegetarian options, and so on. Of the beef there were three different cuts.

The prices were all different and this caused confusion with me. Looking at the different prices there was only £1 difference from the very top price and the very bottom price. Some were just 25 pence less than the top choice. This was added to by the fact that if you wanted a combination of meats, say beef pork and turkey, the guy at the till had to get a calculator out to work out the cost!

After a while we ordered and at the same time asked why this was. 'We like to give people choice' was the reply.

Here's the thing though, with seven choices we were certainly pleased with the variety but the price differences were confusing. What was the point? I suggested to them that they chose a middle ground price between the extreme top and bottom and did a single price to avoid confusion 'I'ts always been that way and it works' I was told. Clearly not listening to the customer.

This is another form of sabotage. People like simplicity and too many choices make your job of choosing difficult. A far more 'user friendly' approach would have been two prices - small and large. You could then choose any meat or combination of and you knew what you were paying.

The food quality was excellent but the feeling of confusion has not left me to this day. Some people looked at the menu and did not order at all.

Action:

Examine every part of your business for sabotage and eliminate it.

Exploiting the Internet

In the 21st century the Internet is the king of all marketing tools. You absolutely, positively, without a shadow of a doubt, *must* embrace the technology we have at our disposal and use it for your business.

Technology is moving so fast today that in five years the Internet will be a totally different beast than it is today. Many people seem to think that the 'net has reached the pinnacle of what it can become but nothing could be further from the truth. This is just the beginning.

The Internet is already destroying the traditional high street. In product terms the Internet makes business transparent: no longer can a business expect to get away with charging 10 times more than anyone else for the same product. The answer to a product's true value is just a few clicks away. This is a good thing; it means the overpriced charlatans of years gone by no longer have the opportunity to rip off the public. So yes, it's good for the consumer – but is it good for business?

Actually, I'd answer that question with a resounding yes! It's not just good for business, it's a terrific opportunity for business, providing that businesses embrace and take the time to learn new principles.

The high street is failing because it is too slow to embrace this opportunity. The shopkeepers of old are burying their heads in the sand hoping this will just go away. Just as the Industrial Revolution changed the way products were made, so the Internet will totally change the way we all buy and interact with businesses across the globe.

The Internet gives any business the opportunity to sell to a global audience. The products or services you have for sale in your high street store you can also sell in Tokyo or Dubai or anywhere there is a need. That is an amazing opportunity for business.

We are all becoming citizens of a global world in which electrons firing over vast distances in the blink of an eye can connect and engage us faster than ever before. As I write this book we are all about to enter an exciting new phase of wearable, Internet-connected devices. Google are about to launch their new technology 'Google Glass' an Internet connected device that you wear as a pair of glasses. This device has the capability to record your every movement and interaction with your fellow human beings and store that information digitally.

It has the ability to deliver 'Augmented Reality', so you can look at a road sign in a Japanese street and the glasses will instantly transform the road sign into English. It will tell you that 100 yards behind you is your friend Joe in a taxi and you will be able to connect to each other's device and chat together about the party you are going to. If you are hungry and want food it will direct you to the nearest Cajun restaurant and even take an order from you so it's ready when you arrive. How's that for marketing?!

Right now the Internet is in its toddler phase – imagine what it will do as an adult.

Any business MUST embrace the available marketing technology of the Internet and learn to turn it to its advantage. The amazing thing about the Internet is that just like individual people, we have individual connections into it. That means that the ability to target different niches of people also exists.

Here's an example. Facebook now has over 1 billion registered users - that's a big number, one seventh of the entire human population have an account with them. Yet in advertising terms I can target all people living in my town with a birthday today and serve them an individual advertising message; something like: 'Hey Julie, come to Joe's tonight and the wine is on the house for your birthday'

Think about that: from one billion users I can target right down to my town and right down to a demographic I can serve them a message that is both relevant and gratefully received for less than the price of a postage stamp. That's marketing power.

If you are ignoring the Internet then wake up and smell the coffee – at Joe's of course :)

Forthcoming books in this series will focus on how to get the most out of these new marketing channels so keep an eye out for them on my author page.

Action:

Investigate marketing channels on the internet that are used by others in your sector

Develop an implementation plan

Just do it already!

I had a chapter earlier in the book about working to a plan, now I'm talking about less planning. 'What is this guy on?' I hear you scream. Planning is all well and good, but too much planning is something you should watch out for.

Many people think of a business idea and then spend days, weeks, months and even years getting ready to launch it. They write spreadsheets, design business cards, come up with a marketing plan, design flyers, talk to lawyers, and go see website designers…yada-yada-yada. They plan and plan and plan without really doing anything remotely attached to their business.

It's an excuse. They are scared, they see this business opportunity but actually making it happen is a big step and they find ways of putting it off time and time again. Some call them 'Wantrepreneurs' because they want a business but never actually make it happen.

Here's the thing. Stop messing about and make it happen. I know it's a bit scary; you are leaping into the unknown. But until you do something, you won't do anything.

There's a scene in the Monty Python movie 'The Life of Brian' where Brian is standing on a rock giving a speech: he's giving the famous 'Look at the birds' lines from the

Bible. Confused, he starts warbling on about birds and lilies and changing what he already said *'He's making it up as he goes along'* came the cry from the audience. It's been a source of much laughter in my home for many years because that's exactly the way that I go into business. I quite literally make it up as I go along. The professional way of saying it is that I adapt to the circumstances that I am faced with.

Having said that, that you do need some kind of guidance as to what exactly you need to make up as you go along. Those answers are in the plan that we began this book with.

When starting in business you must find some very fundamental answer to some very fundamental questions. The very first question is 'Will my product or service sell'? This question is the most important one you will ever ask and it's the first one you must answer.

Before you plan anything, before you start work on that spreadsheet, buy that domain name, go looking for premises or plan how you will deliver this wonderful idea that you have for a business you must establish that there is a need. Once you do this you will know that you have a business to start with.

So forget all of the planning at the beginning, just focus on one thing. How can I find out if this will sell?

There are many ways of testing this - run some ads in your local newspaper, make some phone calls, stand on market stalls - test the market before you enter it.

A short story for you. Back in 2002 I had this great business idea: I was convinced it would sell and was a product that the world needed. At the time I was working in the music business as a mobile entertainer – DJ for want of a better phrase. I needed a way of easily producing invoices for clients that I could do in a few minutes flat. Because *I* needed this service then I figured that others would too.

Here's what I did. I engaged a computer programmer to make me some bespoke software for this purpose. I bought a web domain and some hosting for it and purchased Microsoft Frontpage to design it. I spent literally hundreds of hours learning how to design web sites. I signed with a payment processor and then engaged someone to write me copy for the website. I spent probably three months doing this and finally the day came to launch the site. I submitted my site to Google and Excite (bet you can't remember that one, it was a search engine that was at the top of the game and is still around – if relatively neglected – today.)

I listed my software on eBay and QXL auction sites and waited for the orders to flow in, and they did – all four of them…in three months.

I had committed the cardinal sin of business - I did no research to find out if there was a market for my software and there was none.

Don't make the same mistake. Today it's much easier to find out if there is a market - you can Google any subject and find out if anyone is already selling your idea. If they aren't then resist the temptation to think that you have a global winner – the chances are that it just won't sell. Do your research and make sure that the market for your product is large enough for you to make a living from it.

Here's where the 'making it up as you go along' comes in. If you find you do have something that will sell, then start to sell it. You don't need a spreadsheet to make a sale and once you start making sales you will know what you need to do next. You will start to 'make it up as you go along'

Less planning, more doing.

Action:

Stop messing about and do it!

Psychological Pricing Systems

Let's talk pricing. There are many ways that you can get more money for your product and I'm going to cover two of them here.

The two methods are what I call Price Bracketing and Premium Pricing.

Price Bracketing.

Price bracketing is a method where you show several prices from low to high. This method is commonly used to drive customers towards your – the business owner's – preferred option, and is discussed in the book 'Predictably Irrational' I mentioned earlier. Incidentally, if you want t find out more about the psychology of why we do the things we do then I highly recommend it.

Price bracketing is good because people generally have no frame of reference as to the value of something. If I gave you these two prices which would be the best?

42' Plasma TV $1000

42' Plasma YV $3000

You wouldn't know of course, but what those prices have given you is a reference point as to the value of a plasma TV. Without the first one at $1000 you wouldn't know if the second one was expensive or not. Now, in reality you would never make this offer because there are only two choices. So, let's take a real-world example: magazine subscriptions. *The Economist* once had this on its website (it's changed now, by the way):

Economist Magazine & Internet subscription offer:

- Online version $59 per year

- Print Version $125 per year

- Print & Online version $125 per year

Yes, you read that right - the last two were the same price. So who would want the print only version? It kinda makes the third one a no-brainer doesn't it? Research showed that with this structure **84% went for the top price deal** with just 16% for the low price web only deal. No-one purchased the middle deal.

Now you would think that taking out the middle deal would make no difference but it did.

Online version $59 per year

Print & Online version $125 per year

With this offer 68% chose the lower version and just 32% the higher priced one. The fact that the middle offer made the higher offer a no-brainer increased the sales by double!

I've found what I believe is a better version of this but before I tell you about that I need to cover the second part

Premium Pricing

When buying anything people always WANT the best version they can get, that doesn't mean they will always go for it because of finances but they do WANT it. Look at cars for example - they have many different versions of a car from let's say the S to the SE to the Ghia or GTI for example - everyone wants the top model. All car companies do this with their models but most businesses do not.

If you do not have a premium option then you need one. There are always people that will pay more for your premium rate option but if you do not offer it then they cannot buy it.

Even the cinema chains have now got in the act; Showcase now offer standard seating and premier seating. On top of that they have now launched the Cinema Deluxe with Director's Lounge. Now you can choose standard, premier in a standard cinema, or you can pay a premium and go for The Directors Lounge for the ultimate in cinema. They are almost like a sofa! For my wife and me it cost £26 to go and watch a film – and we happily paid!

So you need premium pricing in your business – and

multiple levels of it.

Going back to our price bracketing above I have found that a choice of three is not as good as a choice of four. Most people want the middle ground in pricing and giving them three often makes it too easy. A choice of four also gives you the option of adding premium pricing for those that want it.

This would be my revised example of *The Economist*'s offer:

Online version $59 per year

Print Version $125 per year

Print & Web version $125 per year

Print & Web Version with Leather binding and gold leaf pagination $249 per year

Take a look at that list - it makes a standard subscription look the weakest, gives an option for the affluent premium buyer and draws the middle ground buyer to $125 whichever he chooses. You may never sell the premium pricing option but that does not matter, it focuses the mind of the prospect on the higher middle.

Think very carefully about your pricing strategy and try to include some of these lessons. Add value, add to the price and make sure you give a frame of reference so people can feel where the value lies.

Whilst we are on pricing I have to say one more thing. Never – but **never** – aim to make your price the USP (unique selling proposition) in other words, never try to be the cheapest in your market. Why? Because it's the easiest thing for your competitors to beat.

There are very few businesses that work on the low pricing angle with the possible exception of a 'dollar or pound shop'.

The use of these two pricing strategies will mean that you sell more of your higher priced options.

Action:

Look into your business and find out where you can offer both bracketing and premium pricing

Don't be afraid of having a high priced offering – if no-one buys then you've lost nothing

Passive Income Streams

This will not apply to every business but if you can do this in yours then your future will be secure.

Allow me to ask a question...

Do you want to work hard forever? Of course you don't!

The way to securing your future profits is to introduce some passive income into your business. An income that comes in month after month whether you do anything or not.

The Internet marketing gurus have refined this into a fine art. Just a few short years ago everything on the Internet was free. If you needed something then you just searched for it and there it was. Following that phase came the 'pay for content' revolution. People would sell you information for a single fee; you would most likely download that information and consume it in your own time.

Today's Internet is a different beast entirely. There are now literally thousands of membership websites. You join up for a monthly fee that gives you access to all sorts of content. Some of that content is software that operates over the net and much of it is in membership sites where people pay a monthly fee to be part of a training course, often delivered via video.

Passive, membership-type income is not only available on the Internet. One of the oldest forms of membership outside of technology is the use of a Gym, people pay up to £100 a month to join a gym and go and use the equipment as a part of that membership. In fact you would find it hard today to find a gym that does not rely on a membership structure.

So what could you do in your business to bring in passive income? If you are in a service industry it's easy, you offer out that service across a whole year in return for a monthly fee. Service companies operate schemes whereby you pay around £20 per month for breakdown cover for your gas boiler. Some Law and Accountancy firms work on a monthly 'retainer' basis. Retainer is just another word for passive income.

You can now buy TV movies on a monthly subscription from companies such as Netflix; satellite TV is built on monthly subscriptions. In retail the likes of Costco operate a membership system selling all kinds of goods.

Passive income provides you with security.

Action:

Try to think of ways that your business could offer a membership scheme. If you are a food outlet you could have a V.I.P club, if you are a hardware store you could have a members' club where they get a certain discount on everything. There are a million different ways to dress it up.

Working *WITH* Your Competition

In the new world of business things have changed. What 'old business' saw as competitors are now seen as collaborators. You must learn to do the same.

Finding new sources of business is hard work. In the past each business would work in isolation, working hard to build up their customer list and holding on to it for dear life. Sharing and working with other companies was unheard of.

Not so in the new world of business. Now, both competing and non-competing businesses in the same sector work together, sharing resources and sharing business.

This will most likely sound alien to you: why on earth would you share your spoils with someone else? Answer: because they will share theirs with you. If you've heard the term 'Joint Venture Partners' (or JVs) that's what this is.

There are two forms of a joint venture partnership. One is where you join forces to promote a product of your own with someone that has a list of ready-made buyers looking for what you have.

Together you promote the product or service and share a percentage of the profits.

This form of agreement is often seen in the Internet marketing world.

As a business owner you have no doubt signed up to an email list in return for some free information. Later they have tried to sell you products and you may have become a customer of theirs. Maybe you bought a video programme, some software or an eBook.

After a while in this relationship the person that you originally bought from may start to offer you services from someone else that is in a similar market. They make recommendations to you based on your interest and the chances are that if you buy the product that they will receive a commission payment.

I've done this many times myself. When I began my book writing career I joined the list of an Internet marketer called Derek Doepker. Derek runs a video training website called 'Kindle Bestseller Secrets' in which he teaches wannabe authors the best way to market their books on the Amazon publishing platform. I bought Derek's course and after a while which he tried to upsell me to a one-on-one consultation method of learning. I declined this. I have no doubts to the quality of the offer; however, being a marketing man I don't feel that I need that level of training.

After being in the 'relationship' with Derek for a while he then began to recommend other training from other people that I may be interested in. If I had purchased then Derek would earn a commission based on that sale. This method of two sellers working together is the typical 'Joint Venture' agreement.

Now, in the case of Derek he even offered me products that were in competition with his own services. He offered me a video course from John Tighe, the author of 'Crush it with Kindle', a bestselling book. These two people are undeniably in competition, offering the exact same kind of training but they still managed to work together. They know that people looking to learn something do not stop at one product but buy several.

This flies wholly in the face of the traditional business model, which is to protect your own customers at all cost. The thing you need to understand is that *this kind of agreement actually strengthens the relationship.* How can you not trust someone who suggests that someone else's product may be better for you than his own? It feels like he is helping you. This generates trust for the seller and trust breeds more sales. Whenever I get an email from Derek I will always take a look and one day may buy from him again.

Can you imagine this in the traditional world of commerce? Let's say a window company saying 'You might like the windows from Joe down the road better than ours' It just doesn't happen, does it? These companies would be wise to think again.

The marketing method I've just been talking about is the

second kind of Joint Venture, one that depends upon trust between two companies to recommend each other's services to their client. The essential ingredient in this arrangement is mutual trust and the willingness to help each other out to an equal measure.

The sharing of your clients with another business does not mean you open up your client list to them. This would be very unwise. The way you do this is that you contact your own clients and tell them about something else they might be interested in. You would always retain your client list but you use it to help someone else.

If this idea fills you with dread then there is an easier way to begin. You form joint ventures with companies in the same general business areas but offering complementary services. For example, a DIY store could JV with a builder. The builder recommends to the client that they buy their raw materials from XYZ hardware store and says if they mention him the store will give them a discount. Similarly the hardware store will advise their clients that if they need the services of a builder they will get a very good job indeed if they employ Joe the builder.

This is the very start of a joint venture and sews the seeds for the future of the partnership. A joint referral arrangement with a complementary business means that you didn't have to work to generate that business lead; it did not cost you a penny piece in advertising. The lead was the builder's client and not yours and he recommended you. The people you send to Joe for building work come to him free and clear. Do you want leads that cost you nothing? Of course you do.

In general terms this is labeled business networking but making it formal between two parties makes it a JV.

An excellent book on true business networking is 'Working the Net' by Simon Bozeat, who also has a full video based training course called 'How to Build a Profitable Business Network' available at www.simonbozeat.com. That recommendation I have just given you is part of a joint venture agreement between Simon and me. He often sends me consulting work from his high-end client base – clients who need my particular style of business marketing skills – and I help him in return.

It's very important that you know and trust the services you recommend to your clients. You have worked hard for your client base and no joint venture should be based on mere lead generation but on a belief that you will be doing your client a good service by this recommendation.

Extending from the business networking side you can then work together to put together offers that benefit both you and your clients. In home improvements for example you could form a JV between a kitchen installation company and a kitchen appliance company. You make a deal whereby you have a kitchen on offer with one company supplying and installing the kitchen and another supplying and installing the appliances.

Now think about this - there is a sacrifice here. A kitchen company can, if they wish, buy the appliances themselves *and make a profit from them.* However, one thing they cannot buy is the appliance company's client list – a list of people that already trust that appliance company, a list that is used to buying from them. What is that list worth to the kitchen company? A lot more than the profits from a few appliances I'll bet.

There is even a case where one company could give another company in direct competition their dead leads. Leads they have tried to sell to but, for one reason or another, the client did not buy. Maybe the client did not like their company or the product, maybe they just did not like the salesperson: we are all different and all have different buttons that need to be pressed when making a buying decision. A dead lead is worth nothing to you but has value to another company that has not yet pitched the client. Use that value to build a trusting relationship and it could pay you dividends.

In the new world of business, companies now work together rather than in competition. This is happening every day, even though it might sound alien to you. Generating business leads all on your own is hard work. By learning to accept that all businesses are in the same boat you can join together to help each other. Everybody wins.

Action:

Ask yourself "Who could *I* partner with?

Think of complementary services that could work with your business. A dress shop could partner with a shoe store, a garden centre could partner with a summerhouse company, and as described above you can even form strategic alliances with competing businesses if you are willing to make sacrifices.

Then make the connections

Systemise Your Business

People that start businesses are no longer just businessmen: they are often entrepreneurs. It's now uncommon for people to start businesses with the intention of operating that business until they reach 65 years old and retire to the old folks' home.

The old way of business was to have a business and pass it down the family line from father to son and then to his son. That's typically why we have small businesses that have been in operation for well over 100 years.

One business in my small town is an electrical retailer. It was started in the 19th century and what was then the owner's grandchild has almost retired from the business and hopes to pass it onto his son, the fourth generation.

The new way of business is that of the entrepreneur. The typical business owner today does not dream of passing the business on through their family but to 'cash out' at some point giving them time either to start new businesses or to spend a few years on a deserted island somewhere in the Caribbean whilst being young enough to enjoy it.

Whichever view you hold yourself does not matter, the question of succession arises in both cases. Whether you are hoping to pass on your business to your family line or if you are looking for an exit plan there comes the actual point where you yourself need to exit the business.

The problem is that most businesses are built around the thoughts and actions of the business owner. The owner actually becomes the business and it cannot survive without the input of the owner. They are inseparable because the owner is the one that has the golden knowledge of how the business works. The business cannot survive without them.

If you are just starting in business or if you are many years down the line you must consider your exit from the business. There is only one thing that can help you do this – it is called systemization.

During the late 1990's I worked for the world's most famous airplane engine manufacturer, Rolls-Royce. The company builds hundreds of gas turbine engines for the airlines of the world every year. These marvels of engineering keep you in the air when you go on holidays or business trips. Every single engine must pass rigorous teasing and each must be reliable. After all you don't want to be half way across the Atlantic when they go wrong, do you?

Rolls-Royce employs over 40,000 people worldwide that look after everything from the supply chain to manufacturing and service. If this company relied on a single person in even one department it could not function.

Rolls-Royce, just like every other aerospace engine manufacturer has vast swathes of documented systems in place. They tell the engineer exactly what size bolt to use, in exactly which hole. It tells him how many turns the bolt must go and how much pressure to put onto the bolt as it tightens. That bolt will be applied the same way every single time on every single engine.

The jet engine is indeed an amazing product made up of thousands upon thousands of components. Each component has its own manual detailing how it must be produced. The company that makes the bolt we spoke of earlier will know exactly how long the bolt should be to within the thickness of a human hair, how many turns the thread must have and exactly how deep each thread must be cut.

Procedures and systems give repeatability. With a procedure in place the exact same bolt can be produced no matter who the machine operator is. If the usual guy is off sick then someone else can open the manual and follow the exact same procedure to produce the exact same quality bolt.

Your business must operate like this too if you ever want to leave it or sell it. Without a systemised business you will never be able to sell it and never be able to pass it on to your family and expect it to continue.

This subject is covered in much more detail in Michael Gerber's great Book 'The E-Myth' if you have never read it then you really should. Michael covers the subject of systemization much more eloquently than I can so I won't be going into detail here. As usual the book is listed on my book recommendation page at http://marketingformugs.com

McDonalds is another great example of systemization. Regardless of your thoughts on the nutritional value of the Big Mac, the fact is that no matter where you go in the world you will have the exact same experience. A Big Mac in China will taste the same as a Big Mac in New York, Washington or Dubai.

The man that took McDonalds to worldwide fame was Ray Croc; he spent years perfecting the process before he embarked on reproducing that experience around the world. That systemisation gave birth to one of the biggest businesses in the world.

The message I am trying to get across is that if you spot a process in your business that cannot operate without you or another specific individual, and then write down step-by-step what has to happen for that process to complete.

Of course, there will always be decisions that have to be taken by someone but if that decision depends on a single person then the process needs to be documented. What had to be in place for that decision to be made? What would have prevented it and why?

This sounds like hard work and I hate to tell you this, but

it is. But do it you must. Ask yourself this question: what would happen to your business if you were unfortunate enough to have an accident and found yourself in a hospital for the next six months? If your business would fall apart then get your procedures written. I can't imagine anything worse than coming out of a coma in hospital to find your business gone bust and your family living on the breadline can you?

Once you have systems in place your business can be sold or passed down and is an asset to you that has value. Without systems it is just a way that YOU do business. It's reliant on the business owner and is non transferable.

Systemise your business: you know it makes sense.

Action:

Buy and read The E-Myth by Michael Gerber

Plan to systemise your business.

Sharpen your saw

Being in business is not something you can just start and allow to run. You must be on top of the latest trends in your sector and using the latest techniques to grow your business.

Sharpening your saw is a metaphor for continuous learning. A woodcutter must keep his saw sharp to enable him to continue with his work. In the same manner you must take time to learn about new ways of doing business and bringing in sales.

There are so many ways to learn new skills. Reading a book (like this one) is sharpening your saw. There are video programmes you can watch and there are MP3 podcasts you can download. CD audio programmes allow you to learn whilst you drive to appointments - it's the 'In-Car university'.

Personally I read a lot. I get through a book every week - that's 52 books a year. Whenever my wife is watching something on TV that has no interest to me I'll get out my Kindle and read some.

I have a recommended reading page on my website http://marketingformugs.com please do take a look as there are some great books on there including the one's I have mentioned in this book.

Conclusion

There are so many things that are changing in the business world today. Just 40 years ago most people were employed by someone else, and many could not even think about having their own business. Today the self-employed are approaching double figure percentages of the workforce.

This book was written to give you some guidelines and to stimulate your mind to consider how you can make more money in your own business. It's not intended to be a business bible; it's here to give useful tips and techniques on how to grow your business.

Future books in the series will cover exciting new marketing channels and other approaches that might help you too.

I really hope that you have found it useful and if you have then may I ask that you **leave a positive review on the Amazon book page.** Your review will help others decide to read this book and I look at every review personally.

You can simply go to this web address

http://bit.ly/7sinsna

Also check out my other books listed here on my author page http://amzn.to/12fClLF

I'm occasionally convinced to help out as a consultant. If you'd like to talk to me about this then drop me an email to glyn@marketingformugs.com

Finally you can learn even more at my Business Blog by clicking here http://bit.ly/glynblog and joining my mailing list

Keep Marketing!

More Books by Glyn Williams

'Small Business Marketing' Series

Book 1:
The 7 Deadly Sins of Advertising
(And How To Avoid Them)
(Amazon - http://bit.ly/7sinsna)

Book 2
21st Century Tactics
(Amazon - http://bit.ly/21stna)

Book 3
20 Great Marketing Channels

(Coming Soon)

Join Glyn's mailing list and read his business blog
(http://bit.ly/glynblog) for more great tips on sales & marketing

About The Author

Glyn Williams was born in Derbyshire UK in 1963. His father, brother and late grandfather were all entrepreneurs and businessmen. For over 20 years worked in sales and marketing and as a radio personality until in 2012 he contracted 'High Grade Dysphonia', the closest you can get to vocal cancer. Laser surgery of the vocal chords followed which solved the problem but left him without his most basic sales tool in full working order.

Life with a diminished voice forced him to look at a new career that was not dependent on the use of the spoken word. In a change of career he became a writer in 2013 and decided to share his knowledge of sales and marketing through books. He has also been a highly respected foreign exchange currency speculator for 12 years.

He continues to live in Derbyshire England with his wife Daphne.

www.ingramcontent.com/pod-product-compliance
Lightning Source LLC
Chambersburg PA
CBHW071612170526
45166CB00003B/1072

* 9 7 8 1 4 9 0 4 4 0 9 9 6 *